Resettle

An authentic guide for those leaving the armed forces and entering the corporate world

Jac Hughes

Copyright © 2017 Jac Hughes

All rights reserved.

ISBN: 1548266914
ISBN-13: 978-1548266912

For The Fallen

Robert Laurence Binyon

With proud thanksgiving, a mother for her children,
England mourns for her dead across the sea.
Flesh of her flesh they were, spirit of her spirit,
Fallen in the cause of the free.

Solemn the drums thrill; Death august and royal
Sings sorrow up into immortal spheres,
There is music in the midst of desolation
And a glory that shines upon our tears.

They went with songs to the battle, they were young,
Straight of limb, true of eye, steady and aglow.
They were staunch to the end against odds uncounted;
They fell with their faces to the foe.

They shall grow not old, as we that are left grow old:
Age shall not weary them, nor the years condemn.
At the going down of the sun and in the morning
We will remember them.

They mingle not with their laughing comrades again;
They sit no more at familiar tables of home;
They have no lot in our labour of the day-time;
They sleep beyond England's foam.

But where our desires are and our hopes profound,
Felt as a well-spring that is hidden from sight,
To the innermost heart of their own land they are
known
As the stars are known to the Night;

As the stars that shall be bright when we are dust,
Moving in marches upon the heavenly plain;
As the stars that are starry in the time of our darkness,
To the end, to the end, they remain.

CONTENTS

Introduction	1
You Are Not Special	11
Use Your Strengths & Self-Develop	18
CVs & Interviews	25
Networking	36
Productivity	44
Be a Leader and a Manager	53
Don't Be an Island	61
Responsibility is Power	68
Over to You	73
Recommended Resources	82

Introduction

"Change is the law of life. And those who look only to the past or the present are certain to miss the future."

John F. Kennedy

An elephant and a dog became pregnant at the same time. Three months down the line the dog gave birth to six puppies. Six months later the dog was pregnant again, and three months on it gave birth to another six puppies. The pattern continued. On the eighteenth month the dog approached the elephant questioning, *"Are you sure that you are pregnant? We became pregnant on the same date, I have given birth three times to six puppies each time and they have now grown to become big dogs, yet you are still pregnant. What is going on?"* The elephant replied, *"There is something I want you to understand. What I am carrying is not a puppy but an elephant. I only give birth to one in two years. When my baby hits the ground, the earth feels it. When my baby crosses the road, human beings stop and watch in admiration, what I carry draws attention. So what I'm carrying is mighty and great."*

Resettlement is not easy.

It is not a decision that should be taken lightly, but leaving the armed forces should not be a choice that you are afraid to make either. Yes it means removing that comfort blanket we become so accustom to, and yes there will be challenging times ahead.

You are going to doubt yourself, your skills and the reasons why you decided to leave. Take it from me, there will be times when you question everything. One thing I can more or less guarantee is that if you want to be successful, however you define it, you **CAN** be. Before you know it you will be looking back with no regrets. The fact that you have spent money on this book shows that you want to help yourself and add value to your new working environment, which is a great start!

I spent just under 7 years in the Royal Navy serving on great ships with amazing people

I knew that I wasn't there for a full 22 year career but I also wasn't sure what was next.

This book is not about me suggesting life outside the military environment is better, this is about helping individuals who want some insight and honesty about the truths of leaving. I wouldn't be where I am without the Navy and will be forever grateful for the experiences my time granted me.

The aim of this book is to simply help; I wanted to write something that someone like me would read and most of all understand. I think resettlement is one of the biggest life changes someone in the armed forces can go through and can seem complicated and daunting.

Write notes, highlight certain words and tear the pages out if that's what you need, but most importantly use this book how you see fit. This is your journey and you **CAN** start to make your own rules.

I never thought I would be writing a book, never mind one about resettlement. The information within these pages will not be for everyone and I can accept that, my only hope is that if you take away just one thing from reading this, let it be that there are opportunities ahead, you just need to take them. You may think some of the things I've written are obvious, my aim is not to be condescending but you will surprised at some of the issues people come across when going through resettlement.

I will be totally honest in the fact that I did not utilise the career transition set up as much as I possibly should have. The admin involved, especially when still serving at sea during my notice period seemed like a burden I did not want or have time to take on. In my opinion, the careers fairs are probably the best and most valuable thing on offer. The careers transition partnership do a fantastic job but I do think certain aspects need to be made easier for service leavers. Applying for a course using Enhanced Learning Credits (ELC) seemed much easier once I had left in comparison to when I was serving, which doesn't make sense to me.

The day I put my notice in I had:

- A decent wage
- One mortgage
- 4 GCSE's
- Some Leadership & Management certificates
- A girlfriend (now wife) who thought I was crazy
- No exit plan

As a write this I have:

- A much better salary
- 3 Properties (2 buy to lets)
- Qualifications I can actually use
- A supportive wife
- The knowledge I can achieve what I set out to do

I have highlighted these points, not as some sort of ego boost, (for most people what I have now might seem pretty modest) but to highlight that you can achieve your definition of success. To me the journey I have been on since handing in my notice in January of 2014 has been a huge learning experience and one I want to use to help others in a similar position.

The message I want to convey is that if you really are ready to leave then it is up to you to make it happen, and make it a success. No one is going to hand it to you (more on this in chapter 2.) This might mean you end up doing something you never dreamed of. My initial plan was to enter the maritime security industry as my trade in the navy was above water weapons, so it seemed like an obvious fit.

Surprisingly, I ended up in IT, firstly within Project Planning and management, now I help teams realise their own potential and have a hand in coaching organisations to become better and more productive. How did that happen? Luck? Chance? Hard work? The truth is like everything in life, a mixture of them all. I was lucky that a chance meeting at a careers fair opened up a conversation about a different career path, but once I made the decision I worked hard to put myself in the position I am in now.

These two rules of silver should be remembered throughout:

1) There are no silver bullets to success

2) Nothing will be handed to you on a silver platter.

I challenge you to ask anyone who has achieved any sort of success, how they did it. They won't give you a short answer, it will be along the lines of hard work, dedication and resilience.

People find that strange because it doesn't sound interesting but it is the truth, the route to success isn't glamorous. It's hard, it can be draining and it takes sacrifice. You need to be prepared for that fact.

The first step is to be open to change, there will be a lot of it and you have to be prepared……

You Are Not Special

"If you don't like something, change it. If you can't change it, change your attitude."

Maya Angelou

The first thing to understand is that no one owes you a job because you have served in the armed forces. This might trigger some people but it is the honest truth and a fact I believe some people need to read. People might tell you it's easy, that companies come knocking on your door and this may be true for some, but the reality is that you are the one that is going to have to initiate the door knocking.

Over 14,000 people leave the armed forces each year. That is 14,000 other people you are in competition with, just from the forces. Never mind over 200,000 graduates and experienced professionals looking for jobs. Not all will want to enter the corporate world but that is still an immense amount of competition and you should be fully aware of these figures. I mention these not to put you off but to act as a reminder. The days of talking to your local drafting office or equivalent about your next job are over.

Whether we like it or not, we all need a dose of reality at times, my serving to you is that just because you have served in the armed forces does not make you special. You have unique experiences, no one will argue with that, but in terms of the job market you could end up becoming disillusioned if you think it will be that easy. Too many people who leave the forces expect to walk into a similar paying role or even higher. The competition for jobs at the moment is intense, you have to realise that there may be a younger or less experienced candidate who a company can pay less, sometimes that person might beat you. It doesn't matter how many sea days, operational tours or medals you have. Business is business and you have to put some of your ego aside.

Yes there are people who land on their feet, or at least say they have, but the truth is in most cases you will have to take a wage cut for at least one year. You have to think realistically.

For those of you who have served 20 years or more, you will be entering a world with every coffee imaginable, Xboxes in offices and a flexible work from home policy. This is the new reality that you need to accept. From my experience corporate veterans will see you as some strange new creature to begin with. Your language, sense of humour, outlook and most of all experiences will be alien to them. This will pass with time but their working life has been vastly different from yours and you are now entering their world. Most will not even know your background, in my case a lot of people thought I was a graduate. I would be lying if I said this didn't grate on me at times, how dare they call me a graduate? I've done more in my life than they ever will… blah blah

blah. The fact is that if they want to know they will ask and honestly, most people won't care what you did in your previous job, just the same way you might not have been interested in what a new joiner did on their last draft, post etc.

There is a balance to be struck however, those unique experiences will have forged your personal values and ideals. Don't lose sight of these as they will be a key strength in establishing yourself in your new environment.

Your insight will be valued, and businesses accept an outside perspective is needed in an ever-changing climate. The confidence you have in yourself will shine through and it will be noticed.

In my opinion, the biggest strength of someone entering the corporate world from the armed forces is their different perspective. Think of all the demanding and extreme environments you may have been in. All of these experiences give you a unique outlook.

When things go wrong in the corporate world people will lose their heads quickly, you will find yourself questioning what all the fuss is about and comparing situations you have been in. Your perspective should give you confidence and it will eventually filter into your new colleagues.

This is not to be confused with arrogance that you have been in situations more important, to your new peers they will have worked hard to be where they are and if you start to undermine them it will be hard to claw back any rapport you have built.

Quick wins

- **You are unique not special**
- **Leave some of your ego behind**
- **Hold onto your values– they will serve you well**

Use Your Strengths and Self-Develop

"Absorb what is useful, discard what is not, add what is uniquely your own."

Bruce Lee

The transferable skills you have acquired during your time in the forces are almost limitless, due to the nature of the environments you have been in, you could probably turn your hand to most things.

Firstly take a step back and reflect on what you really want to focus on. You will have spent years in and out of theatre, the odds of you wanting to become a software developer who writes codes all day are pretty slim. This is not to say that you couldn't if you had the motivation and interest, but those people are few and far between.

However, I would put money on the fact that your people management skills are up there with the best. With some training and experience a well-paid HR role would not be out of sight. The same goes with Project Management, the planning and execution skills you have picked up, probably without even realising would be a major asset to any business.

Those who leave the forces are rough diamonds and I personally would never fully smooth them out. It's the roughness that sets you apart, the fact that you won't mind getting your hands dirty or in a business sense, having a difficult conversation with a team member. I had no idea about project management before I jumped in head first, but I soon came to realise that my approach would be one of common sense and purpose. To my surprise this seemed like a new concept in some companies, again I go back to the perspective we have on the world and how work can be carried productively.

Once again, you need to strike a balance between staying in your comfort zone and choosing to push yourself further. During and after your resettlement period you are going to need the motivation to self-develop. I don't mean the stereotypical self-development of standing in front of a mirror and chanting about how powerful you are, I mean development in the area you find yourself in. You are a new comer and will need to take advantage of all the resources available for you to upskill and keep up to date in whatever field you enter.

Books, podcasts, blogs, articles, LinkedIn and even searching for information on Google. All of these are at your disposal and can be accessed for free from your mobile phone. Use them to your advantage and get yourself ahead of the competition.

You can pass all the exams in the world but if you do not continue to develop your knowledge you will soon be left behind. There is always someone else willing to work that tiny bit harder and you need to be able to keep up.

Choose the path you want you to go down and pursue, research and master it to the best of your ability.

There is an approach called F.O.C.U.S which means Follow One Course Until Successful. This is exactly what you need to do, try and become the best you can be in one area and expand from there. If you want to become a Project Manager, book yourself onto a Project Management course. There are numerous available using enhanced learning Credits.

Whatever route you choose, you need to aggressively take action to achieve the results you hope to achieve.

Don't feel this decision should be rushed but it should be made all the same, the clarity of knowing what you want to pursue will provide you with the focus to get started.

The times we live in mean the information is out there, you just need go and find it. As time goes on you will start to enjoy learning, especially if the area you are learning about interests you (I was absolutely horrendous at revising in school.) It is only now I am in a job I love that self-development and learning has become an important part of my life. Use this to your advantage, as your motivation will be greater than someone who has been in a company for a number of years. Your fresh approach along with new ideas will only benefit you.

Self-development is a journey that has no end point, you will have to constantly reflect on how far you have come. I have no doubt that I will look back at how this was written a year from now and cringe at some of the content. Will there be anything I can do about it? Not really, but we can all learn from where we have been.

Quick Wins

- **Perspective is key**
- **Don't underestimate your transferable skills**
- **Self-development is key to gain an edge**
- **Your willingness to get your hands dirty will set you apart**

CVs & Interviews

"One important key to success is self-confidence. An important key to self-confidence is preparation."

Arthur Ashe

CVs

While quite a short chapter, it is probably one of the most important.

Everyone will have an opinion on what makes a good CV, you need to understand what makes a great one. Your CV will in most cases be the first impression that a hiring manager or recruiter has of you. If you don't make it count, the self-doubt will creep in after a while of not hearing back about jobs that you have applied for. You will be amazed at the amount of times I have read a CV that says something like... I am an enthusiastc person with an eye for detail. Notice the spelling mistake in enthusiastic? You have to get the basics right in terms of spelling and grammar. The fact that this person wrote that they have an eye for detail and included a spelling mistake would mean their CV would go no further. Harsh maybe, but recruiters and hiring managers haven't got the time to sift through CVs with mistakes on. You could be an outstanding candidate only to have it ruined by an oversight.

Keeping with the time theme, make sure your CV is no longer than two pages, it needs to be engaging but to the point, they don't want your life story. If you are applying for a specific role or job then tailor you CV to that job. A generic CV is great for a job fair but when you are looking at something particular, you have to focus on what you can bring to that individual business or role.

As a service leaver you will write and talk in a certain way, keep in mind that most people looking at your CV won't understand military terms. You are going to need to turn your military language into something that a civvie can relate to and compare with other candidates.

The above might seem simple but they are things that service leavers get wrong time and time again. If you don't feel confident in writing your own CV, there are companies who are able to help, and in some cases you can pay to have it written for you. There is nothing wrong with this but keep in mind that you don't want to be just another CV in the pile, you want to get across who you are to the person reading it.

Quick Wins

- **Spelling and grammar are essential**
- **No longer than two pages**
- **No military language**

Interviews

"Success consists of going from failure to failure without loss of enthusiasm."

Winston Churchill

The old saying of piss poor preparation leads to piss poor performance rings true in regards to interviews. You can't go into an interview underprepared, you will get found out very quickly. You might not have had an interview for years, which is why it is so important to be prepared.

If you fail to prepare properly for an interview, you are basically self-sabotaging. As well as the quick wins at the end of this chapter keep in mind the points below.

Most times the application process will start off with an informal chat with a recruiter before going onto the next stage in which the hiring manger will become involved.

The interview format doesn't matter, be prepared and remember:

What's on your own CV

Study your CV like you are revising for an exam. You would be surprised at the amount of people who forget what they have written about themselves. It is easy to stumble when asked a question under pressure. Get someone to ask you questions beforehand if needed.

Don't be late

Enough said

Don't be too early

Arrive an hour early and it looks like a) you don't have anything else to do and b) you are poor at time management. Neither are a good look.

Know the company you are interviewing for

Again, it sounds obvious but if you are only looking at the homepage of the business, you have to ask yourself if you actually want the job. Research the company you are interviewing for. In most cases you will only get asked basic questions about the business but it is key to have some idea about how they work or what they have achieved. You will want the floor to swallow you if you are asked something about the place where you supposedly want to work and haven't got an answer. Do some digging in the news and on LinkedIn, it will only look good on your behalf when you are up to date with company affairs.

Buy a suit

I don't care if you are interviewing for an unpaid internship, you must turn up in a suit. It shouldn't even be a consideration not to. The amount of times I've seen people ask if they should wear a suit for an interview is unbelievable. You are there to project the best version of yourself, with the aim of acquiring a position you want. In short, suit up!

Be Confident

Confidence is key during an interview, like I mentioned you are there to project yourself in a positive manner. They have invited you there for a reason, something stood out in your CV and now is your time to build upon that. Look the person who is talking to you in the eye, look like you are engaged in what they are saying.

Depending on where you are interviewing for will dictate the sort of questions you are going to be asked. Some will be structured and formal, others will be less formal and open. Don't let the latter put you off, you are more likely to say something you regret in an open conversation so tread carefully while ensuring your personality is coming across.

Don't be afraid to use examples from your military experience, as long as it is related to the question, I guarantee the interviewer will have never heard an example like yours. This is where your unique experience comes into its own. Military examples of team work and working in high-pressured situations make you stand out compared to someone with slightly more corporate experience. It will make you memorable when it comes to decision time.

Stay Calm

The most important thing is not to over think the process, the people who will be interviewing you are still human, and they will have the same insecurities you do. Be calm, confident and most importantly yourself. No job or company is ever worth changing who you are for. The person you are has gotten you where you are today, so you must be doing something right.

There are enough corporate robots out there without you becoming one.

Quick Wins

- **Do your research and be prepared**
- **Suit up no matter what**
- **Be confident without coming across as arrogant**
- **Be yourself**

Networking

"Do one thing every day that scares you."

Eleanor Roosevelt

LinkedIn

LinkedIn should become your new favourite social media platform, I can't recommend it enough. As soon as your decision to leave has been made, create your own profile and become an active user. You will soon find yourself connecting with like-minded individuals who can point you in the right direction. Most recruiters and hiring managers will look you up and a well-constructed LinkedIn profile will go a long way. You can even apply for jobs directly so the importance of having a well-structured profile is priceless.

It is not just about looking for jobs and people either. LinkedIn has an endless supply of articles, blogs and videos to enhance your self-development.

Most of the content is written by motivated professionals from their chosen field. The benefit of this is that they are writing from a real time, up to date perspective. The groups and forums are full of enthusiastic people who are more than happy to answer questions and discuss every topic that is written about.

All it takes is to use the search bar and you will find hundreds of recruiters with active roles that need filling. Don't just click the connect icon, make the effort to send an introductory message. It might take some time but a personal message will go a long way. Recruiters remember people who they like and will keep your name at the forefront of their mind for any roles they feel suitable.

Try and work with them and they will work with you, they are there to make a sale and will do their best for you if you do likewise.

A pissed off recruiter will soon let others know if they feel you are difficult to work with.

LinkedIn has the potential to become one of your most powerful tools, use it well and your inbox will soon start to fill up.

I challenge you to set up your profile **today**.

LinkedIn Quick Wins

- **Browse profiles to get a feel of what you think will work for you (obviously don't copy and paste someone's summary)**
- **Don't use your nickname, it will put people off straight away**
- **Use a headshot, not a picture holding two pints of Guinness**
- **It is not Facebook, posting cat videos is not advised**

Talk to People

Social Media is great and should be used and taken advantage of. However, nothing will ever replace getting out there and talking to people. Careers fairs, meet-ups, workshops and networking evenings are just some to think about.

We live in an age where connecting with people is easier than ever, reach out to someone, buy them a coffee if you have to, you never know where it might take you.

The easiest and fastest way to improve yourself is to reach out to someone who is at a higher level than you are and ask them how they did it. The most successful people in the world started somewhere.

Spending time with those playing a bigger game than you, will only be of benefit and give you confidence that you can achieve the same. Listen to what they have to say as it will be valuable, write notes about how they achieved certain things if you need to.

Don't be afraid to ask questions, if they have said yes to a conversation with you they will be happy to answer your queries.

You are the average of the 5 people you spend your time with.

The above theory has been recycled many times but that is because it is true. If you are surrounding yourself with people who want to improve themselves and move forward with their lives, it will only enhance your mind-set.

If you are spending time with people who are questioning your decisions and not being supportive, you may want to think about the amount of time you are spending with them.

This doesn't mean they are bad people, I am sure they have your best interests at heart but ultimately the negativity will only fuel any self-doubt you might already be harbouring.

All of this may be something that is totally alien to you and that's fine, just understand that the whole resettlement process will take you out of your comfort zone as you move away from the safety net of the forces.

You are going to have to put yourself out there and begin to network with people outside your normal circle. This shouldn't be too difficult, just think back to all the times you joined a new unit, ship or base without knowing anyone.

One of the strengths of being ex forces is that you will tend to treat people with respect from the off. It won't matter if you are speaking to the top of the corporate food chain or a receptionist, the respect will be there and that will only serve you well.

Quick Wins

- **Don't rely solely on social media**
- **Accept you are going to have to talk to people you may not want to**
- **Make every encounter count**

Productivity

"Simplicity boils down to two steps: Identify the essential. Eliminate the rest" –

Leo Babauta

The honest truth is that you will be used to in short 'getting shit done'.

Another truth is that the corporate world is full of people who are busy but unproductive.

The information within the rest of this chapter should help you avoid becoming a busy fool.

80% of the value is in 20% of the work.

As shocking as that might seem if you think about it, it actually makes sense. There have been countless studies around productivity and the ratio still stands the test of time.

80% of the revenue is generated by 20% of customers.

80% of complaints come from 20% of customers.

80% of quality issues occur with 20% of our products.

Those are just a few examples of how it works and the 80/20 rule is something that will act as a useful reference when you start to feel overwhelmed with work.

There was a study based on how much time people spent on e-mails within a department. An individual received 511 e-mails on a weekly basis, they sent 284, that's almost 160 coming in and out each working day. Even if this person was highly efficient and processed each e-mail within 30 seconds, the total time used would still amount to around an hour and a half per day.

235 of the emails were from people within the company, that being close to 46%, and colleagues cc'd them on 172 emails. This volume of emails was slightly above average, but even some senior executives were receiving close to 550 emails and sending almost 800 in a week. With an average of 32 words per email (around two sentences).

By calculating average typing speed, reading speed, response rate, volume of emails, average salary, and total employees, the total spent on emails was around 1 million dollars per year.

1 million dollars for people to process emails.

I shared this because this is without doubt the single biggest strength you should utilise. The most noticeable thing I have noticed about ex-forces moving into the corporate environment is that they are able to point out where time is being wasted within a few weeks of being in a company.

The most underused but highly effective productivity tool is the notepad and pen. Start writing what you notice down and start to eliminate waste as soon as you can.

In terms of individual productivity, there are a number of great planners on the market, one of which I have recommended at the end of this book. It is amazing what writing things down can do for your productivity, it can also help you reflect on your week's achievements.

One tool I find useful is using MoSCoW prioritisation. It can be broken down into:

Must do tasks, business critical, tasks with an impending dead line etc.

Should do tasks, task that are important but not critical.

Could do tasks, tasks of low priority that add little value.

Won't do/will do next time tasks, tasks that have no impact to the business and have no deadline.

The aim is to do this on a Monday morning before you start the working week, clearly defining which tasks must be done first.

Try and do one or two must do tasks per day before moving onto lower priority tasks. It is vital you start on the hardest task first. These are often the ones you do not want to do and on another day would avoid. Get them done and your day will go so much better. Your sense of achievement will increase and you will be ready to move onto the next task. Put them off and the anxiety of knowing that they are hanging over you will become a large load to bear.

You will ultimately find your own way of working and there will be an element of trial and error. Eventually you will find a system that works for you. Once you do stick to it.

You can always build on it and look for improvements. If something doesn't work just remove it.

There is a Japanese word called Kaizen, which when googled reads as *a Japanese business philosophy of continuous improvement of working practices and personal efficiency.*

All this really means is trying to improve one thing each day.

One small thing every day. That's potentially 365 improvements in both your work and personal life each year. This concept alone can improve your mind-set and even if you are having the worst day ever and wish you were back where you feel comfortable, you can at least hold onto that one improvement you achieved.

Be Committed

There is a story that is told when describing commitment in business, it is based on a chicken and a pig:

A Pig and a Chicken are walking down the road.

The Chicken says: "Hey Pig, I was thinking we should open a restaurant!"

Pig replies: "Hm, maybe, what would we call it?"

The Chicken responds: "How about 'ham-n-eggs'?"

The Pig thinks for a moment and says: "No thanks. I'd be committed, but you'd only be involved."

The question is, what do you see yourself as?

There are many chickens in the world, but good pigs are hard to come by.

Become committed to productivity not busyness.

Quick Wins

- **Be productive not busy**
- **Remember the 80/20 rule**
- **Do the most important tasks first, always**
- **Add one piece of value each day**

Be a Leader and a Manager

"If your actions inspire others to dream more, learn more, do more and become more, you are a leader."

Simon Sinek

Examine the definitions in the below table.

Do you consider yourself a leader or a manager?

Leaders	**Managers**
Focus on people	Focus on things
Do the right things	Do things right

Motivate their employees	Direct their employees
Influence those around them	Control those around them
Wants to earn respect	Wants to be liked

Being solely one or the other might well work but incorporating both will benefit you and those around you.

What does this mean?

Corporate culture is changing.

There are endless materials on the subject of leadership and management along with the differences and similarities between the two. Most will have been written by far more intellectual and wealthier people than myself and I do not claim to know it all.

The one thing I can say with confidence is you need a vision of the type of leader or manager you would like to be. The table is not prescriptive, you do not have to be one or the other.

The modern workplaces requires you to be aware of when someone needs support, as well as knowing when you need to push to achieve a goal. It is not black and white.

There are 3 simple evolutions of management that can be broken into the following:

Management 1.0 - Pure command and control (Doing the wrong thing)

Management 2.0 - Lack of leadership and structure (Doing the right thing wrong)

Management 3.0 - Managers managing the system for people to thrive (Doing the right thing)

The days of individual cubicles/offices and a suit being the standard uniform are slowly but surely coming to an end. Businesses are changing with the times and that comes with its own leadership challenges. People want be self-governing so they can master their trade, without being micro-managed. If you find yourself in a leadership or managerial position, letting go of command and control may be difficult. However, if you focus your efforts on managing the systems and creating an environment for those you are leading to grow and organise themselves, the improvements and results will speak volumes.

This style of leadership is sometimes referred to as servant-leadership. This means that you serve your team so they can produce quality work.

This type of leader is happy to be in the background, letting the team take all the credit for the work they achieve. While at the same time being the leader they can turn to when needed.

This is a complete mind-set shift for some people, but it is a skill that can be practised and mastered over time.

You should bear this in mind during any interviews you attend, as it is still quite a new concept that hiring managers will be keen to hear about.

The millennial generation attract a lot of negative attention in regards to being entitled and expecting an easy life. In some cases this may be true but do not neglect the fact that just because these people, who you will be working with, are young, does not mean they do not add value.

The changes within businesses have come from the need and want for change. People do not work as effectively when command and control is in place. I am not suggesting you stop dressing well, grow a beard and let your peers 'get away with murder'. But you have to understand that the environment you are entering is vastly different from military hierarchy. You might find the CEO of a business walking through the office in jeans, a hoodie and flip flops. Again, I stress that I do not want to come across as condescending but the fact is, due to your rank, some of you reading this will have only needed to raise your voice slightly or look at someone in a certain way to get what you wanted.

The modern corporate management tree is becoming flatter and ideas and inputs are coming from the bottom up as well as the top down.

There are still boundaries in place but in a modern office environment they are harder to distinguish. The military experience you have will provide you with the confidence to lead effectively, but keep in mind subtle changes you may need to make in your approach.

Quick Wins

- **Command & Control should be used with caution**
- **Visualise the type of leader/manger you would like to be**
- **Reflect on your experiences with good and bad leaders**

Don't Be an Island

"Ask for help. Not because you are weak. But because you want to remain strong."

Les Brown

I can honestly say my period of transition from the Navy into civvie street was the hardest and most draining time I have been through. Saying that depression crept in would be an insult to people who genuinely suffer with mental health issues, but there were times where I didn't think I could carry on with the course I had worked hard to get on, and eventually the role I would be moving into. I made decisions that were out of character and I felt like I didn't belong in my new environment. I wanted to be back with my mates in surroundings I was used to.

I was good at being in the Navy.

Would I ever get my head around this new language?

Part of this was down to imposter syndrome. At first I believed I did not belong in my new environment, it was full of well educated, middle class people who I never thought would accept me. I often wondered how I ended up sitting at a desk within Lloyds Banking Group. I now know that these thoughts that plagued my mind couldn't be further from what people were thinking, and now I appreciate the skills I have to offer.

Those thoughts haunted me for a while and to an extent still do, but nearly 3 years down the line the negative thoughts and feelings do not occupy my mind as frequently. I realise I was given a role for the value I could add, along with the fresh perspective I could bring to the table.

I hope you have more confidence in yourself than I did, but even if you don't admit it, there will be times when you ask yourself why you are doing what you are doing. This is normal, don't think that it isn't. The key thing is not to shut people out, your support network, be it family or friends are there for you. They might not understand what you are going through or feeling and nor should you expect them to. Just remember that they want to be there, tell them you are having a bad day or finding new skills hard to grasp.

For some reason men are considered worse than women in regards to talking about their feelings, but it is not just men who suffer in silence. Women who have served in the forces are considered just as mentally strong as men and from the outside this may be true. The fact is that mental health does not discriminate, male or female.

You have to put your ego aside, if you don't talk to someone it will only spiral out of control.

It is not a sign of weakness, although I would be a hypocrite if I claimed to be the best person at verbalising my feelings. It comes with time and once spoken about your problems will be easier to consolidate and deal with.

It is going to be hard, some find it easier than others but I can almost guarantee that everyone finds a certain aspect difficult.

Keep in mind that you didn't know much about military life during basic training and look how far you have come and what you have achieved since then.

There are also times that no matter how positive you try and remain, life will serve you a blow. Sometimes all any of us can do is ride the storm and hope that things get better. There is no getting away from that fact and I would be foolish to write otherwise.

As Winston Churchill said "If you're going through hell, keep going."

Give Yourself a Break

The biggest and maybe the most important bit of advice I can give is to take time out, don't become obsessed with deciding your next step.

Take a step back or a few days break from thinking about it. The harder you try and force something, the harder it will become. After a few days break you will feel refreshed and motivated to carry on.

Don't neglect those around you, they will still need you to be present in their lives. Don't become overly selfish in your pursuit to find what you are looking for. I imagine some of you will be leaving the forces to spend more time with your family.

What is the point if you are only there in body but your mind is elsewhere?

Yes, your resettlement is about you and what you want to achieve, but a balance has to be struck for your sake, as well as those around you.

Quick Wins

- **Try not to shut people out**
- **Reflect on past achievements to help build confidence**
- **Take time out when it is needed**

Responsibility Is Power

"Don't judge each day by the harvest you reap but by the seeds that you plant."

Robert Louis Stevenson

There is a concept called Extreme Ownership, a former US Navy Seal called Jocko Willink wrote a book about it. The concept is basically that no matter where we are in life, our own decisions have taken us there, good or bad.

The excuses we all come up with are irrelevant and non-productive. If you think of times where things have gone wrong I bet there was a decision you made that could have been different.

In the same breath, when things go wrong, we have all looked to someone else to harbour blame.

This is a routine that needs to be broken, especially during your resettlement period.

Some things are out of our control, we can however choose how to react to every situation.

You need to understand that it is your responsibility to make resettlement work for you. There is plenty of help out there, but it is up to you to take what is offered, the help and most importantly the job opportunities won't come to you.

You will feel like you are getting further with the process if you take responsibility for it yourself, having information spoon fed will only delay things.

Do your own research and make your own opportunities. A job isn't going to just appear, like I said earlier you are in competition with thousands of other people, so it is up to you to get yourself where you want to be. That might mean doing courses in the evening or at weekends, but a year from now it will be worth it once you and your family are in a financial position that is the same or better than it was while you were serving.

From the moment you hand in your notice or decide to leave, that 1 year count down begins.

1 Year

12 Months

365 Days

8760 hours

525,600 Minutes

31,536,000 Seconds

Broken down it might seem a lot but that time will soon go and you will be handing in your ID card.

Don't delay taking action, even if that is just starting your CV or looking at courses. You don't have to decide straight away, but the little things you start will help you in the long run. Write down at the start of each month what you would like to achieve, and take the time to be honest with yourself in regards to the progress you are making. Obviously you are still going to be doing your day job and possibly even away from home, but there is nothing stopping you from taking learning material with you to read when you have some spare time. Again, taking small, simple steps will only help you in the long term. Procrastination will hinder your plans and time will slip away.

The sooner you start to take responsibility for your resettlement the easier you will find it. If you leave it to those last few months you will only have yourself to blame. It is not worth doing it to yourself or the people who may be relying on you.

Quick Wins

- **Start planning straight away**
- **Identify what you want to learn**

Over to You

"Actions speaks louder than words but not nearly as often."

Mark Twain

I want to start this chapter by sharing a story by Admiral William H. McRaven told during a speech at the University of Texas. It highlights the power of small achievements.

Every morning in basic SEAL training, my instructors, who at the time were all Vietnam veterans, would show up in my barracks room and the first thing they would inspect was your bed. If you did it right, the corners would be square, the covers pulled tight, the pillow centered just under the headboard and the extra blanket folded neatly at the foot of the rack — that's Navy talk for bed.

It was a simple task — mundane at best. But every morning we were required to make our bed to perfection. It seemed a little ridiculous at the time, particularly in light of the fact that we were aspiring to be real warriors, tough battle-hardened SEALs, but the wisdom of this simple act has been proven to me many times over.

If you make your bed every morning you will have accomplished the first task of the day. It will give you a small sense of pride, and it will encourage you to do another task and another and another. By the end of the day, that one task completed will have turned into many tasks completed. Making your bed will also reinforce the fact that little things in life matter. If you can't do the little things right, you will never do the big things right.

And, if by chance you have a miserable day, you will come home to a bed that is made — that you made — and a made bed gives you encouragement that tomorrow will be better.

If you want to change the world, start off by making your bed.

Do not take for granted the little wins, you will need to hold onto them during tough times.

No one else can make a success of your civilian life but you. It doesn't matter how many books you read or courses you attend, the motivation has to come from within. No one can motivate you. They can inspire you to take action but after that initial feeling fades, it rests on your shoulders to move forward.

Corporate jobs can sometimes receive a negative reputation, but I can only speak of positive experiences. There are still days when I don't think I am getting anywhere and become frustrated, but is that any different from any other job in the world? You will be surprised at how well you can fit in to your new environment once you have settled in.

I have been lucky in that I found a career that I have a genuine passion for. I believe anyone can find the type of job they want, but don't be surprised if it is something you have never even heard of. Be open to something different, something that is going to keep you interested and motivated.

Be prepared for people to take the piss about some of your choices. This will more than likely happen because they haven't got the balls to leave themselves. They would rather be unhappy than make a success of something else, and their only outlet is to project that onto you. I imagine some grief will fly my way because of this book but I would choose to be writing this at home, in a job I love over being told what to do by someone with as much leadership ability as a slug.

The first and simplest thing I can advise for you to do is get out a notepad. Write down what you think you might be good at, what your skills are and most importantly, what you think you are going to enjoy. Beyond serving your full time there is a reason you want to leave the forces, so why go into something you are going to dislike just as much or more?

Get it all down on paper and reflect on what you have written, I bet you will be surprised with how much you actually write on the page. Start researching jobs that match your actual interests, believe it or not you can find a job that you will enjoy.

I truly believe that anyone leaving the armed forces can carve themselves a successful new career.

Patience is key, you will not achieve everything within the twelve month resettlement period. The services available to you go beyond one year and there are so many online groups for ex-forces to communicate you won't find it hard to find support.

Use everything at your disposal and most importantly, don't be afraid to ask questions to acquire the information you need.

Once you have made the decision to leave and taken the steps needed, you have opened the door to endless job possibilities.

All you need to do is put yourself in a position to find them.

Everyone's resettlement experience will be different, don't be put off if someone seems to be ahead of you, the odds are they will be trying to improve in another area that you are thriving in. Support each other as you have done throughout your military career.

This is an honest account about my experience along with the information I have picked up along the way. I wanted to write a book that highlighted some key situations that you will come across during your own resettlement process.

I welcome any feedback on this book and I hope it has been of some value to you.

If you have any questions then please look me up on LinkedIn and I would be more than happy to help if I can, or point you in the direction of someone who may have more knowledge.

I hope you have gained some value from reading this and I wish every single one of you all the luck in the word.

Now pick your notepad and start **YOUR** own journey.......

Recommended Resources

These are some of the books, podcasts and online groups that may help you as you go through resettlement and beyond.

Books

Mindset with Muscle – **Jamie Alderton**

How to be fucking awesome – **Dan Meredith**

I get shit done planner – **Dan Meredith**

SCRUM – **Jeff Sutherland**

Eat That Frog – **Brian Tracey**

Deep Work – **Cal Newport**

The Subtle Art of Not Giving A Fuck – **Mark Manson**

Start With Why – **Simon Sinek**

Make Your Bed: Little Things That Can Change Your Life...And Maybe the World – **William H. McRaven**

Podcasts

The Body and the Beast

Fitness – It's A State Of Mind Podcast

London Real

TED Radio Hour

The Gary Vee Audio Experience

Online Groups

FDM Ex-Forces Programme – LinkedIn

Printed in Great Britain
by Amazon